Aesop's

Retold by Jenny Dooley & Chris Bates

Stage 1 Pupil's book

Express Publishing

Published by Express Publishing

Liberty House, Greenham Business Park, Newbury,
Berkshire RG19 6HW, United Kingdom
Tel.: (0044) 1635 817 363
Fax: (0044) 1635 817 463
email: inquiries@expresspublishing.co.uk
www.expresspublishing.co.uk

Design and Illustration © Express Publishing, 2007

Colour Illustrations: Terry Wilson

Music by Ted & Taz © Express Publishing, 2007

First published 2007
Eighth impression 2016

Made in EU

ISBN 978-1-84679-369-1

CONTENTS

hare

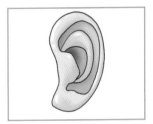

ear

leg

run

wind

strong

4

"My name is Harry Hare.
My ears are very long,
and I can run just like the wind
because my legs are strong!"

5

tortoise

shiny

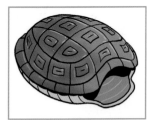

shell

short   tall

thin   fat

"My name is Timmy Tortoise.
I've got a shiny shell.
My legs are very short and fat
and I can't run so well."

come on

slow

go

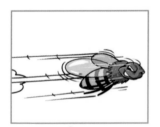

fast

8

"Oh come on, Timmy Tortoise!"
"I'm really slow it's true!
But anywhere I want to go,
I'm just as fast as you!"

funny

dare

race

lunch time

"That's very funny, Timmy!
Just race me – if you dare!"
"Let's have a race tomorrow, then,
at lunch time Harry Hare!"

Activities A-C

Which one is the fastest –
the tortoise or the hare?
Which one is the fastest?
Who can win the dare?

Chorus: Get ready, get set
and run, run, run!
Get ready, get set!
Get ready for some fun!
Get ready, get set!
Get ready for some fun!

Which one is the favourite –
the tortoise or the hare?
Which one is the favourite?
Who can win the dare?

Repeat Chorus

13

animals

gather

sun

midday

put up his hand

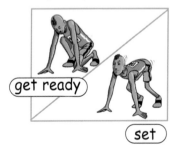

get ready

set

The animals all gather
under the midday sun.
Then Freddy Fox puts up his hand.
"Get ready, set, and RUN!"

15

look

far ahead

near

16

"The Hare is running quickly!"
"Poor Timmy is still here!"
"But look! The hare is far ahead!"
"And Timmy's nowhere near!"

see

win

18

"Come on, Timmy! Do your best!"
"Please, Timmy! Make our day!"
"We want to see you win this race,
but Harry's far away!"

it's getting hot

huge

tiny

dot

"Harry Hare's still running fast."
"It's getting very hot!
But where is Timmy Tortoise now?
Is he that tiny dot?!"

Activities D-E

21

behind

sleep

bed

under

apple tree

hour

"He's very far behind me –
I know what I can do!
I'll sleep under this apple tree
for one hour, maybe two!"

23

Don't Stop Until You're at the End!

No one is the winner
until they cross the line.
You're half-way there, Harry Hare,
but there is still some time!

Chorus: Don't stop until you're at the end!
           Rest at the finish line!
           Don't stop until you're at the end!
           Don't stop until it's time!

Repeat Chorus

Don't stop until you finish!
You'll soon be on the line!
You're half-way there, Harry Hare!
Don't sleep until it's time!

Repeat Chorus x 2

24

pass by

snore

before

after

26

Timmy Tortoise passes by.
"Harry Hare is snoring!"
"There isn't very far to go!"
"You'll get there before him!"

dream

fast asleep

gulp down

big

small

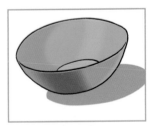

bowl

ice cream

28

"Harry Hare's still fast asleep!"
He has a funny dream –
he sees the tortoise gulping down
a big bowl of ice cream!

29

wake up

look around

look for

find

30

Harry Hare wakes up at last
and starts to look around.
He looks for Timmy everywhere –
he's nowhere to be found!

Activities F-G

31

finish line

"I can win the race today!
There's still a lot of time."
"Can you see the tortoise?
He's near the FINISH line!"

light

sad

tear

face

34

Harry runs as fast as light,
but Timmy wins the race.
Poor Harry Hare is very sad –
the tears run down his face!

cheer

party

"Now everyone is cheering!"
"Timmy's number one!"
"It's time to have a party now!"
"Come on! Let's have some fun!"

remember

walk

stop

cross

"Slow and steady wins the race,
remember that next time!"
"Just keep on walking!" "Never stop!"
"Until you cross the line!"

Activities H-I

39

Song

Slow and Steady

When something that you really want
seems like it's out of reach,
just think about the tortoise –
here's one thing he can teach:

Chorus: Slow and steady wins the race,
so just keep pushing on!
Run to win! Don't give in,
and you'll be number one!

Keep looking at the prize ahead –
your luck can always turn!
Just think about the tortoise –
here's one thing you can learn:

Repeat Chorus x 2

ACTIVITIES

Activities for pages 4-11

A Look at the pictures and match them to the words.

leg

tortoise

lunch time

wind

hare

shell

B Look at the pictures and (circle) the correct words.

0
  a fat
  (b) short

1
  a fast
  b tall

2
  a strong
  b shiny

3
  a thin
  b fat

4
  a strong
  b thin

5
  a funny
  b slow

C Can you find these words in the puzzle?

~~come on~~	race
dare	run
ear	shell
funny	slow
go	tortoise
leg	wind

```
t  r  u  n  l  i  w
o  m  e  a  s  l  n
r  s  h  e  l  l  e
t  g  o  a  o  e  f
o  r  c  r  w  g  u
i  a  w  i  n  d  n
s  c  o  m  e  o  n
e  e  d  a  r  e  y
```

42

D Look at the pictures and fill in the missing letters to complete the words.

0   w_in

1   pu_ up

2   gat_er

3   _ee

4   get _eady

5   l_ok

6   it's ge_ting hot

7   se_

E Look at the pictures and fill in the puzzle.

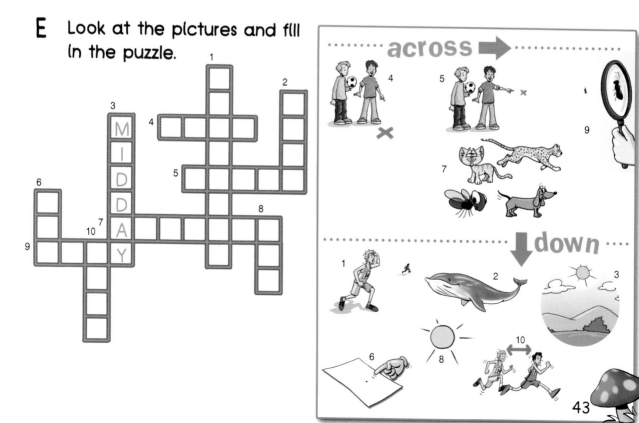

across ➡

down

43

F Look at the pictures and letters and write the words.

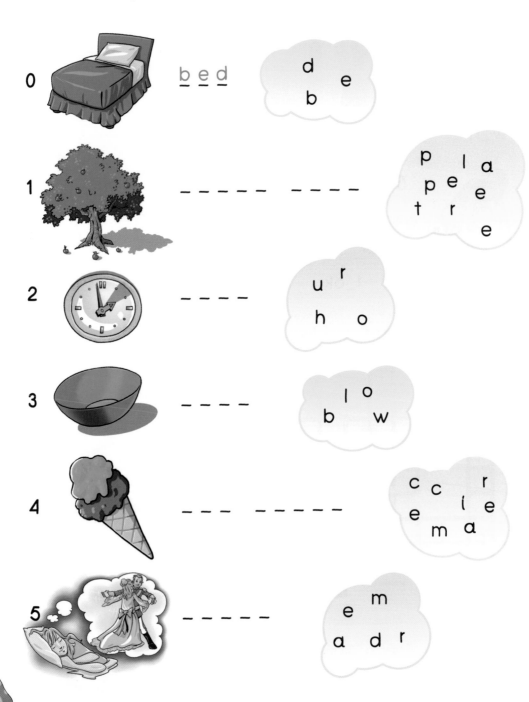

0   <u>b e d</u>   d
          e
       b

1   _ _ _ _ _   _ _ _ _   p   l a
                        p e   e
                        t   r   e

2   _ _ _ _   u r
            h   o

3   _ _ _ _   l o
            b   w

4   _ _ _   _ _ _ _ _   c c   r
                      e   i e
                       m a

5   _ _ _ _ _   e   m
              a d r

G Look and read. Write yes or no.

0 The man is looking around.  ....yes....

1 Jenny is waking up.  ....

2 Grandpa is snoring in bed.  ....

3 Sam is gulping down his food.  ....

4 A girl is passing by a boy.  ....

5 Timmy is sleeping.  ....

H Look and copy.

He remembers this house.
They are crossing the street.

He is walking.
They are cheering.

0

They are
cheering.

2

....

....

1

....

....

3

....

....

I Circle the words.

finishline tearface partylightsad

J Write the words and match them to make rhyming parts.

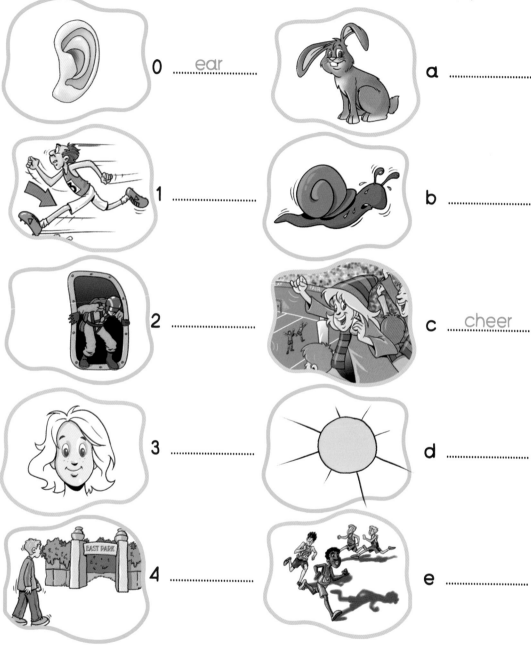

0 ......ear......

a ....

1 ....

b ....

2 ....

c ......cheer......

3 ....

d ....

4 ....

e ....

0 ..c..   1 ....   2 ....   3 ....   4 ....

K Look at the pictures and read the sentences. Put a tick (✓) or cross (✗).

0 This is a sun. ☒

3 This is a bed. ☐

1 This is a tear. ☐

4 This is a tortoise. ☐

2 This is a party. ☐

5 This is a dream. ☐

48

L Look and write. Then, tick (✓) the odd-one-out and say.

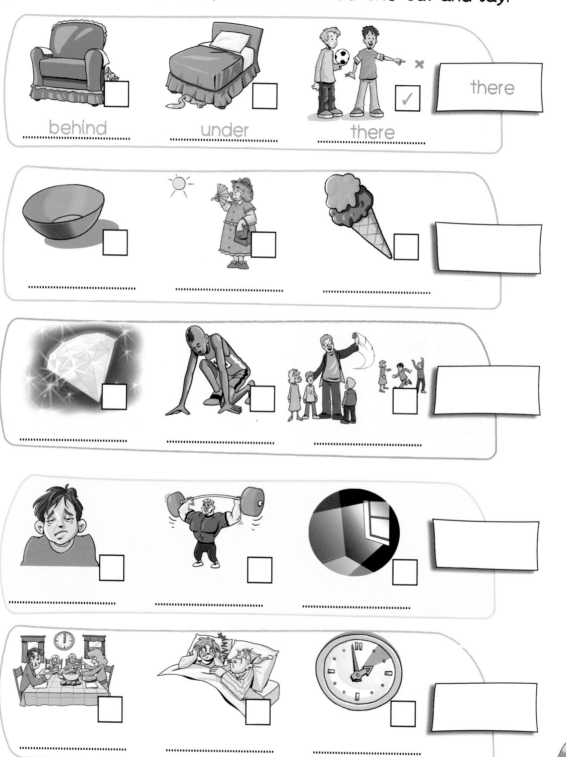

behind .... under .... ✗ ✓ there .... there

....

....

....

....

M Who says what? Listen and write.

Freddy Fox

Harry Hare

Timmy Tortoise

Mr Skunk

---

0 "I can run just like the wind
because my legs are strong."

Harry Hare

---

1 "My legs are very short and fat
and I can't run so well."

....

---

2 "Get ready, set, and RUN!"

....

---

3 "Harry Hare's still fast asleep!"

....

---

4 "I can win the race today!
There's still a lot of time."

....

---

5 "Slow and steady wins the race,
remember that next time!"

....

N Look at the pictures. Then, write the words to complete the sentences.

0 He is ....snoring............ in bed.

1 He is .... around.

2 He is .... down his food.

3 He is .... for his ball.

4 He is .... in a race.

5 She is .... in her bed.

O Read the number key and colour the picture.

1	light blue	**8**	light brown
2	blue	**9**	dark green
3	yellow	**10**	light green
4	orange	**11**	black
5	red	**12**	grey
6	light orange	**13**	white
7	brown	**14**	pink

▶ Now, let's act it out!

Actors:

Harry Hare	Miss Owl	Mr Skunk
Freddy Fox	Mr Snake	Mr Frog
Mr Bear	Timmy Tortoise	Miss Deer
Mr Eagle	Mr Squirrel	Miss Duck

Narrator: One, or as many Ss as necessary, dressed as forest/farm animals.

Scene 1 (In the forest)

Harry: My name is Harry Hare.
My ears are very long,
and I can run just like the wind
because my legs are strong!

Timmy: My name is Timmy Tortoise.
I've got a shiny shell.
My legs are very short and fat
and I can't run so well.

Harry: Oh come on, Timmy Tortoise!

Timmy: I'm really slow it's true!
But anywhere I want to go,
I'm just as fast as you!

Harry: That's very funny, Timmy!
Just race me – if you dare!

Timmy: Let's have a race tomorrow, then,
at lunch time Harry Hare!

Song: Get Ready!

Which one is the fastest –
the tortoise or the hare?
Which one is the fastest?
Who can win the dare?

Chorus: Get ready, get set
and run, run, run!
Get ready, get set!
Get ready for some fun!
Get ready, get set!
Get ready for some fun!

Which one is the favourite –
the tortoise or the hare?
Which one is the favourite?
Who can win the dare?

Repeat Chorus

Scene 2 (In the forest)

Narrator:	The animals all gather under the midday sun. Then Freddy Fox puts up his hand.
Freddy:	Get ready, set, and RUN!
Mr Squirrel:	The Hare is running quickly!
Miss Duck:	Poor Timmy is still here!
Miss Deer:	But look! The hare is far ahead!
Mr Snake:	And Timmy's nowhere near!
Mr Skunk:	Come on, Timmy! Do your best!
Mr Bear:	Please, Timmy! Make our day!
Miss Owl:	We want to see you win this race, but Harry's far away!
Mr Frog:	Harry Hare's still running fast.
Harry:	It's getting very hot! But where is Timmy Tortoise now? Is he that tiny dot?! He's very far behind me – I know what I can do! I'll sleep under this apple tree for one hour, maybe two!

Song: Don't Stop Until You're at the End!

No one is the winner
until they cross the line.
You're half-way there, Harry Hare,
but there is still some time!

Chorus: Don't stop until you're at the end!
                Rest at the finish line!
                Don't stop until you're at the end!
                Don't stop until it's time!

Repeat Chorus

Don't stop until you finish!
You'll soon be on the line!
You're half-way there, Harry Hare!
Don't sleep until it's time!

Repeat Chorus x 2

Scene 3 (In the forest)

Narrator: Timmy Tortoise passes by.

Miss Owl: Harry Hare is snoring!

Mr Squirrel: There isn't very far to go!

Miss Deer: You'll get there before him!

Mr Skunk: Harry Hare's still fast asleep!

Narrator: He has a funny dream -
He sees the tortoise gulping down
a big bowl of ice cream!

Harry Hare wakes up at last
and starts to look around.
He looks for Timmy everywhere –
he's nowhere to be found!

Harry: I can win the race today!
There's still a lot of time.

Mr Eagle: Can you see the tortoise?
He's near the FINISH line!

Narrator: Harry runs as fast as light,
but Timmy wins the race.
Poor Harry Hare is very sad –
the tears run down his face!

Freddy: Now everyone is cheering!

Mr Squirrel: Timmy's number one!

Miss Duck: It's time to have a party now!

Mr Bear: Come on! Let's have some fun!

Timmy: Slow and steady wins the race, remember that next time!

Mr Bear: Just keep on walking!

Miss Owl: Never stop!

Mr Skunk: Until you cross the line!

Song: Slow and Steady

When something that you really want
seems like it's out of reach,
just think about the tortoise –
here's one thing he can teach:

Chorus: Slow and steady wins the race,
so just keep pushing on!
Run to win! Don't give in,
and you'll be number one!

Keep looking at the prize ahead –
your luck can always turn!
Just think about the tortoise –
here's one thing you can learn:

Repeat Chorus x 2

PHOTOCOPIABLE MATERIAL   **59**

◗ Props

Props	SCENE 1	SCENE 2	SCENE 3
whistle	✓		
flags		✓	
banners		✓	✓
red flag		✓	
a big bowl of ice cream			✓
a gold medal			✓
party hats			✓

Word List

The words in colour are presented in the picture dictionary of the story.

a lot of	do your best
after	dot
all	dream
animals	ear
anywhere	everywhere
apple tree	face
as fast as light	far ahead
at last	fast
because	fast asleep
bed	fat
before	favourite
behind	find
big	finish
bowl	finish line
can	funny
cheer	gather
come on	get ready
cross	go
dare	gulp down

Word List _____

half-way there	maybe
hand	midday
hare	name
have fun	near
have got	next time
here	nowhere
hour	number
huge	party
ice cream	pass by
it's getting hot	poor
it's true	put up
just like	quickly
keep on	race
leg	really
let's	remember
light	rest
long	run
look	sad
look around	see
look for	set
lunch time	shell
make our day	shiny

short	there
sleep	there is time
slow	thin
slow and steady	tiny
small	today
snore	tomorrow
so well	tortoise
soon	under
start	very
still	wake up
stop	walk
strong	want
sun	where
tall	win
tear	wind
then	winner